all seasons pass

grieving a miscarriage

all seasons pass

grieving a miscarriage

Martha Manning

SORIN BOOKS   Notre Dame, IN

International Standard Book Number: 1-893732-08-8

Library of Congress Catalog Card Number: 99-67516

Cover design by Michele Wetherbee
Illustrations by Nicky Oritt
Cover Photograph by
 Toshio Naka/Photonica

Printed and bound in the United States of America.

In memory of Catherine

Sophia came to her one night. She came to deliver her from the darkness of the night and the darker nights to come. She did not recognize Sophia, but in some ways she had always known her—in moments, in fragments, in glimpses. Sophia came to her when she felt alone. Alone with a baby inside. A baby who couldn't wait. A baby who began in a mother who was readier in heart than she was in body. A baby who is now gone.

the dream

She dreamt about a scene from her childhood—her grandparents' beach house. It was a typical New England beach whose terrain often changed radically with the seasons and the years. She remembered that as a child she arrived at the beach late at night—too late to see what the beach looked like that year. She always woke very early the next morning, ran to the seawall, and scanned the beach for changes. She loved that scene and it brought her a gentle peace in the times she let herself imagine it.

It came to her differently this time, as she lay there exhausted, in the space between awake and asleep. There were two people in the scene this time, herself and an old woman in a yellow slicker walking along the beach. She had never seen the woman before, and yet there was so much about her that was familiar.

Her white-blonde hair was pulled back with wisps falling around her face. And her hands were like her mother's—artist's hands. It was strange. She looked a little like her mother, her husband's mother, a little like her grandmothers—all in a diffuse way that could not fit words.

The old woman seemed to know her. She smiled and greeted her by name. Puzzled, she asked, "How do you know my name?" The old woman laughed and replied, "Child, see that lighthouse?" Of course she saw the lighthouse—Minot Light. She loved that lighthouse. At night she loved to sit on the sea wall hypnotized by the rhythm of its blinking light. When she was a little girl, her mother told her that it spelled out in code the words, "I love you." As an adult she wasn't sure if that was really true, but it was one of those things she didn't really want to know the truth about—in case it spelled something else, or worse, nothing at all.

"Yes," she replied. "I've known that lighthouse all my life."

"Well, child, I'm Sophia, the keeper of the lighthouse. I've known you all of your life."

As she tried to figure that out, the old woman motioned her toward the shore, held out her hand, and said, "Let's walk." They walked slowly and silently, watching the water, watching the beach. In the silence she was overcome with sadness and began to cry. The old woman stopped walking and asked why she was crying. She began to sob and said, "I'm so sick and scared. I feel so alone and I'm not strong anymore. I don't understand what's happening to me. I can't make it better and no one else can either."

The old woman smiled at her and said, "Child, look closely at the beach. Has it always looked like this?"

She was puzzled. Why would the lighthouse keeper ask such a stupid question? But she tried to respond.

"No, it's never the same. It's always different."

"How is it different?"

"Well, it differs with the seasons, with the years."

"Tell me about the differences."

"When the winter has been gentle the sand is so clear and smooth you can see crabs scurry along the beach. When the winter has been harsh it is littered with thousands of rocks and shells and it takes all summer to toughen the bottoms of your feet so that you can finally walk barefoot. Some storms bring seaweed, jellyfish, junk. And some storms wreck the boats and the moorings close to the shore. It's always different. That's why I like it."

"Tell me about the storms," said the old woman.

"They're fierce. The ocean goes wild and its power is awesome—

terrible, but at the same time, beautiful. I loved watching the storms from the sea wall, standing barefoot with a slicker over my bathing suit. My grandmother would call me to come inside and watch behind the safety of the picture window. But she didn't understand. I was safe on the sea wall. It was exhilarating to be in the middle of it all—in danger and safety at the same time."

"Well, child," the old woman said, "the beach has been through gentle and fierce weather. It changes constantly, but it is always here. No matter what happens to it, every year the ocean and the beach are here for you. Do you understand?"

The young woman wasn't sure. What was there to understand?

As she hesitated, the old woman asked another question. "Tell me about the beach house. Has it always been the same?"

"Oh, no. This is the fourth house I've known since I was a child."

"What happened to the houses?"

"They were destroyed in hurricanes and blizzards. But my grandparents always rebuilt them. This fourth house was designed in a different way. The other houses were destroyed by the force of the water rushing through them. The new house was made in two sections connected by a glass hallway. It was designed so that in a bad storm the ocean could have a way to rush through it without doing any major damage."

"What do you think of this house?"

"At first I didn't like it at all. It was so different from the houses of my childhood. It's not a traditional New England beach house. But it really is the most creative of all the houses. It's also withstood some very hard winters."

"Yes it has," answered the old woman. "Now do you understand?"

"What is this woman trying to tell me?" thought the younger woman. "Why doesn't she just come out and say what she wants me to know instead of playing this game with me?"

They walked on farther. The old woman bent over and picked up something nestled in the rocks. She held it open in her hand for the young woman to see. It was a piece of glass—smooth, green, opaque. As children they called it sea glass and competed with each other to see who could find the most beautiful pieces.

"Child, what is this?"

"It's sea glass," the young woman answered impatiently.

"And how does it become sea glass?"

"A bottle of glass breaks on the beach and then the sea and the rocks and the sand wear down the jagged edges, take away the shine, and put a crystal texture on it."

"I want you to understand about sea glass."

"What's to understand? I already told you what I know."

"Here, I want you to hold it, rub your fingers around the edges, feel it against your cheek."

The young woman explored the piece of glass. It was cool in her hand, and the edges were curved and smooth.

"Okay," she said, and tried to hand it back.

The old woman laughed and said, "Child, you've just begun to know this glass."

She placed it back in the young woman's hand again and said, "Look at it, smell it, taste it."

She looked at it closely and saw the different textures of green. She held it up to the sky and watched the colors play with the glass and the water. She saw ridges—places where the glass was more worn than others. She smelled the glass. It smelled like air, salt, sand, and water—all at the same time. Then she put the glass to her tongue, tasted it, and instantly felt that she'd been engulfed by a wave of sorrow.

"What does it taste like, child?" asked the old woman, looking directly into her eyes.

The young woman began to weep and answered, "It tastes like tears."

The old woman put her arms around her and held her close. And she said softly in her ear, "Yes child, that's the sea. That's the sea. . . . Do you understand now?"

She still wasn't sure she understood, but she was beginning to know that the old woman was telling her something important.

They stood in silence for several moments.

Then the old woman said, "There is something I want to tell you that you will need to remember. Listen to me carefully and keep this with you: This is a season . . . and all seasons pass."

Then the old woman said, "It's time for me to go now."

The younger woman grabbed her hand, pleading, "Please don't leave me alone."

The old woman laughed again and answered, "Child, just because you feel alone doesn't mean you are alone. I have known you always, and now you know me. You can never be alone."

"But where are you going? Where can I look for you?"

"Look inside yourself and look all around you."

"Yes, but where can I find you?"

"You aren't listening to me. Look inside you. Look around you. And if you forget where to look, you can always look toward the lighthouse and let the light guide you."

The younger woman began to protest with another question, "But I don't underst. . . ."

"Child, you don't have to think about it. Just let it happen."

She ran her hands across the young woman's cheeks and wiped away her tears. Then she kissed her forehead, turned, and walked slowly toward the light.

She awoke in a post-surgery haze—disoriented, groggy. What was this room with the sharp lights and strange noises? What were these needles and tubes? When did this day begin? She felt confused and terribly thirsty. Then she heard someone saying her name.

There was a nurse sitting by her side, helping her to awaken. Then she realized where she was, and why.

She turned to the nurse and asked, "There's no more baby?"

And the nurse replied, "No honey, the baby's gone."

The tears stung in her eyes and began to fall down her face, but her arms were at her sides, hindered by IVs and blood pressure cuffs, and tucked under blankets. The nurse bent over her and gently wiped the tears from her nose and cheeks. And then the nurse took chips of ice and put them one by one on her tongue. Nothing had ever tasted so good. She remembered the lighthouse woman, and knew she was not alone.

"This is a season," she whispered to herself, "and all seasons pass."

In the days that followed, she found comfort in communion with many women—some close friends, others whom she hardly knew. They shared their losses—of infertility, of pregnancies, of babies.

She experienced the paradox of sensing her strength at a time when she felt most broken.

And slowly she began to know what the lighthouse keeper had told her. She understood about the seasons of the beach: that the sweet, warm, gentle weather must alternate with the fierce and powerful storms. In its own way, each gives something to the beach.

She understood about the beach house: that its beauty is in its durability. And that its durability comes, not from offering resistance to the power of the ocean, but in finding a way for the water to pass through, thereby saving it, and letting it stand strong.

She understood about the sea glass: that tears and sorrow are as natural as the sea. And that the cool green light of the glass doesn't come without cost. That what changes it from a worthless bit of discarded glass involves getting knocked around in the sand and the rocks, and letting the ocean smooth over the jagged edges. Patiently. Slowly. Over a long long time. So that one day, a child walking on a New England beach will see a green light sparkling on the shore and she will bend down, pick it from the rocks, and claim it as her treasure. And in that moment, the transformation is complete.

The sea's sorrow becomes the child's joy.

Sophia brings up her own children,
and cares for those who seek her.
Whoever loves her loves life,
those who wait on her early will be
   filled with happiness.
Whoever holds her close will inherit
   honor,
and wherever they walk the Lord
   will bless them.
Those who serve Sophia minister to
   the Holy One,
and the Lord loves those who love
   her.
Whoever obeys her judges aright,
and whoever pays attention to her
   dwells secure.

If they trust themselves to Sophia,
  they will inherit her,
and their descendants will remain in
  possession of her;
for though Sophia takes them at
  first through winding ways,
bringing fear and faintness to them,
plaguing them with her discipline
  until she can trust them,
and testing them with her ordeals,
in the end Sophia will lead them
  back to the straight road,
and reveal her secrets to them.

  (see Ecclesiasticus 4:11-18)

All Seasons Pass is the story of a miscarriage—mine. I was the young woman who expected that life should be "fair." If I just tried hard enough and did everything perfectly, I believed that I would be in control of my life. But life has all kinds of ways of knocking that fantasy out of your system. For me, miscarriage was one of those ways.

The story of Sophia is true. In the grip of a high fever, with no sleep and difficulty breathing, I lay in bed dreading the coming night. As I tried to slow and steady my breathing, I dropped like an elevator to a less conscious state. I wasn't asleep. It was a feeling of being wide awake, but transported someplace else. A place where I felt whole and relaxed, where everything was going to work out in the end. Sophia came to me just as I have described.

At the time, I knew I was as close to a hallucination as I ever wanted to be, and that other people might think it was just too weird, so I only told one person. Then, after I lost the baby, and Sophia's words echoed and comforted me, I shared the experience with others.

For a long time the psychologist in me wanted to find a way of defining Sophia's visit. Maybe it was intense imagery, vivid fantasy, or a hypnogocic hallucination. But Sophia resists categorization, and so shall I.

a personal history

At the age of twenty-five I decided it was time to have a child. I was in the middle of a Ph.D. program and my husband, a social worker, had just gotten his first job, making all of $10,000 a year. It never occurred to me that there could be barriers between my wish to become pregnant and actual conception. And there weren't. After my husband and I had my pregnancy confirmed and announced it to our friends and family, many people asked the same question, "How long did you try to get pregnant?" to which I would shrug and answer, "About ten minutes." From my current perspective, it was an innocent, but arrogant, remark.

My pregnancy was—in the words of my medical chart—"unremarkable," although it didn't always feel that way. I couldn't believe how much a person could vomit on a steady diet of tea and toast. And then, when I felt hungry again, I couldn't believe how much a person could eat in a single day. My daughter arrived one week past her due date. I encountered my first "failure" in labor when I couldn't speed up dilation, and then finally passed the twenty-four-hour window, after which a C-section was indicated. I got a wretched infection, and in the haze of a high fever, tremendous difficulty nursing my newborn, collapsing veins, and postpartum depression, my arrogance began to fade. Fast. My illusion of total personal control over childbirth bit the dust.

Seven years later, following the requisite degrees, academic appointments, and entries on the résumé, we decided to go for number two. My OB cautioned that with my increased age, I should expect it to take between three and six months to conceive. Again, it took about ten minutes. But that is where the similarity between the first and second pregnancies ended.

Within a week of confirmation of the pregnancy, I developed a severe case of relentless bronchitis that stole my sleep and complicated access to the usual treatments that would help me but harm the baby. I was tortured with severe anxiety attacks, sleeplessness, and agitation. I wanted the baby so much, and with every passing week I wanted it more. But there were also times when I didn't want it, when I wanted to take it all back, change my mind, wait till I was healthier. But all that changed when I heard the baby's heartbeat, and then the next week as I watched my husband and daughter hear it. I was still sick. The term "morning sickness" was a joke. *All day*, every day, I had nausea that didn't much care if I was driving along the highway or shopping in the grocery store. I embarrassed my daughter more times than she or I care to remember or count.

On the day of an appointment for a sonogram, I wore the first of several new maternity dresses I'd bought, and realized I felt better. On the cusp of my second trimester, I decided I'd finally turned a corner. I was oblivious to the technician's concern as she traversed my abdomen trying to get a good shot of the baby. She had to call in someone else. And then someone else. I was blissfully ignorant during the entire process. Finally, the doctor came in and studied the sonogram screen. He fiddled with dials and sighed. Then he came over and said softly, "We can't get a heartbeat." In a level of denial I still can't believe, I told him not to worry because we'd heard the heartbeat several times already. He looked into my eyes and repeated himself. I still didn't know what he was talking about. Then he took my hand, motioned toward the sonogram screen, and said, "Martha, the baby is dead."

I was convinced there was a mistake. But there wasn't. Ten hours later I went to the hospital for a

D&C. For several days I felt dazed, like a tornado or earthquake had ripped through my body and my life. Later I felt angry—at myself, and at God for not hanging in there with me, and for not protecting my baby. It was like God had pulled the rug right out from under me. I was deeply sad and convinced that I could never go through something like that again. It was a time of tremendous isolation—even from people I loved. I searched for ways to observe the loss, and there weren't any. Even women who'd been through miscarriages weren't too helpful. Women of my mother's generation, who had large families, tended to be more philosophical, "It's for the best." "It's God's way of taking babies who will not make it, or will suffer profoundly if they're born." Women my age and younger who are much more into the "tech-nology" of pregnancy always asked, "Do they know why you lost the baby?" And some women actually had the nerve to offer their theories.

Six months later, I did go through it again. Again, getting pregnant was the easy part. I wasn't nearly as sick as the time before. But nine weeks into the pregnancy, I sensed that something was wrong. There was an excruciating week of back-and-forth about whether I was still pregnant or had an imminent mis-carriage to deal with. After tests and sonograms, my doctor said there was no viable pregnancy, and I had another D&C. This time I was numb. I made the decision that I would go through no more miscarriages, that I was lucky to have one child. I have known women who have gone through six or eight miscarriages, finally to have a good pregnancy and a healthy baby. But I have also known women to lose many pregnancies and never have a baby.

My one child, now twenty-one, is the greatest blessing of my life. My experience of my five brothers and sisters is so valuable that I fear for my daughter—that she will lack the family I so treasure. I worry about the burden that two old parents might have on an only child. I still keep track of my lost children. I know how old they would be now and wonder what would have been if I had three children.

There are still times when I am startled to find myself physically aching in my heart. Often, when I give myself a moment to reflect, I realize again that after all this time my body still remembers what my mind forgets. It may be a due date or the anniversary of a miscarriage. Now, after all this time, when those images and memories arise, I am able to let myself just think about them, to say, "Oh, that's what the pain is." Then I give myself a couple of minutes to cry, to clear my throat and blow my nose, to realize that I'm all right. I can move on. My husband and daughter both tense up when we watch a program in which an expectant mother delightedly studies her baby on the sonogram screen. That one's still a bit too close for me. But I can rejoice with women I know and love for whom a sonogram picture is a link to the extraordinary—a healthy growing baby who will make it to birth, transporting its parents' dreams into the most beautiful of realities.

the sorrow of miscarriage

It is estimated that between ten and twenty percent of all *known* pregnancies end in miscarriage. Because the rates of miscarriage are so high, there has often been tremendous insensitivity about the pain of such loss. Our culture has historically offered little recognition that miscarriage is a traumatic event in the lives of potential parents. And, because our culture doesn't truly register the loss of a pregnancy as anything more than an accident of nature, there are few contexts in which miscarriages are formally observed.

The long-standing and varied traditions in which other types of death are observed allow for a series of steps through which mourners progress. These traditions focus on allowing for the expression of suffering, the sharing of that suffering with others, the giving and receiving of love and support. They offer ceremonies that provide mourners with a shared way of being together in their pain, and then to commemorate the deceased in concrete ways that enable the mourners to continue to experience an emotional or spiritual connection to the lost one.

But many people don't see the loss of a pregnancy as a death. As frustrating as this is, it's easy to understand how it happens. Pregnancy loss, especially in the first trimester, is often "invisible." Friends, relatives, and co-workers who find out about the miscarriage before they ever knew about the pregnancy can find it difficult to imagine grief over something they can't see. The irony is that expectant parents know about, see, and hear their developing babies earlier and earlier as technology becomes more sophisticated. A pregnancy may still be invisible to the outside world, but hearing a heartbeat, seeing a tiny being on a sonogram screen, knowing the sex, choosing a name, and then receiving the most incredible of "previews"—the photographed sonogram image—all intensify the process of attachment. The technology that helps us know we are pregnant early and provides us with many different types of information about our babies contributes also to widening the isolating gap between a couple grieving a lost pregnancy and the people around them.

Pregnancy is *never* invisible for a woman. The way her body snaps to the attention of a totally different commander is an awesome, albeit sometimes uncomfortable, process. Tough-as-nails women find themselves crying at telephone commercials. Energetic women find themselves so fatigued that they could lay down in the middle of traffic for a nap. For many women, getting through an hour without vomiting can feel like a major lifetime accomplishment. Very quickly, women experience changes in the way they look. Some of these changes go against norms of what is considered attractive in our culture and lead women to reevaluate and reprioritize what is important to them. The list of what you aren't allowed to do during pregnancy grows—and entails giving up a lot of things fast, or starting to do things you hate.

Pregnancy alters a woman's center of gravity—literally. But there are so many other changes as well, and so much is happening "invisibly." So when a pregnancy is lost, almost every aspect of a woman's life is turned upside down *again*—except this time there is no baby at the end of it all. Her body and mind still feel pregnant—without the baby.

control and blame

Ours is a culture that treasures the illusion of control. We are told in bold and subtle ways, in all forms of popular media, that we are masters of our own health. The assumption is that if we do everything "right," we will not have a heart attack, get breast cancer, or gain weight. While taking personal responsibility for our health is basically a positive thing, the hidden message—that doing A, B, and C will most certainly accomplish D—can be a negative. Especially when things go wrong. Then it's a perfect set-up for blame. The bookstore shelves are full of guides about how to "do" pregnancy right. *But you can do everything right and still lose.* And when you lose it is easy to blame yourself or feel the sting of others' "helpful" but essentially blaming comments. After a personal disaster, it's natural that we scan back in our memories to pinpoint a cause, to identify where things might have gone wrong. The implication is that if we can isolate that *one* cause, we can avoid it in future pregnancies, thereby guaranteeing positive outcomes.

With my first miscarriage I punished myself with thoughts that it happened because I worked so hard, that I wimped out and took prescribed antibiotics for severe bronchitis. Other people filled in the gaps, saying gently things that screamed in my ears, "Maybe next time you should lay off the Diet Coke," or the more blatant, "I told you that you should stop playing racquetball." I felt angry at them, and angrier at myself. What if they were right? What if this was my fault?

distance

We live in a time where we are struggling to come to terms with ethical questions about the beginning and end of life. These issues go far beyond abortion or euthanasia. The ambivalence became painfully clear to me when the "baby" I was joyfully expecting and announcing instantly changed to the "fetus" following my miscarriage. Peoples' attempts to spare me further pain by speaking about my loss with distance undercut my confidence about the rightness of my distress. No one says, "I was expecting a fetus and I lost it." It sounds like a package didn't arrive in the mail. People don't get it. But that should never make you question the depth of sorrow and suffering that you feel.

"I know you mean well, but . . ."

Other cruelties come disguised in a different form of helpfulness. Often the things that are said may be true, it's just that the timing is especially insensitive. Following my first miscarriage I stopped counting the number of people who said something like, "At least you have one child. Be grateful for that." It was an awkward position to have childless friends struggling with infertility who sometimes had difficulty summoning up much sympathy for my loss. My guess is that if the situation had been reversed it would have been similarly difficult for me. It is incredibly important to count and celebrate our blessings, but it is equally important to register and observe our losses. Blessings don't cancel out losses. A rich life requires the co-existence of the two.

Many people find it so painful to deal with loss in the present that they immediately jump to the future. They often spout the "get right back on the horse" philosophy. "You can have loads more children." "This happened to my sister and then she had twins!" On the other hand, people might advise you to stop right now, or that next time you should consult with this specialist and "here's the phone number. . . ."

give grief its due

If there's one thing I've learned from my miscarriages and other serious reversals it's that *you must give grief its due*. No matter what anyone tells you, the loss of a pregnancy is a huge loss. It is the death of a baby and the death of a dream. There is no one way to grieve. The quick-fix mentality about "healing" and "getting closure" after a loss is ridiculous. As if one intervention, one ritual, a specific amount of time or support can speed it all up, make it end faster. Closure is a myth, perpetuated unfortunately by people in my own profession. It is naive to think of a major loss and assume that one day you'll just wake up and say, "OK, that's over. It's all behind me. I am no longer in pain." There is acute grief where the pain invades your house, and whether you like it or not, has the run of the place. Over time, it takes up less space. But if you kick it out too early or pretend it's not there, you're in for trouble. For me "closure" or "resolution" about loss has nothing to do with ending my sorrow. I've found over time that I needed to give sorrow a room in my house, a space to exist. The pain grows muted over time, but it will never disappear. And I don't want it to. Those children will always exist in a place in my heart that is theirs alone. I could never crowd them out. The bittersweet sadness I feel when I go to that place is the rent I pay for the privilege of keeping those babies alive in my life.

there's no right way to grieve

What is helpful to a wife might be torture for a husband. For some people talking is cathartic. There is an almost ritualized story that develops, and in the telling, healing begins. For other people the storytelling, the explaining, the overwhelming amount of human contact (even when it's helpful) can feel assaultive. I remember being appalled before my own miscarriages by a friend who went back to work the day after her miscarriage. I mistakenly assumed that her going back to work was a sign that this loss had not devastated her. What I learned was that working was her way of managing, her way of coping. When I treated a family in which a newborn had died, each parent and

52

each child had a different way of dealing with it. The problems came in the assumptions they each made about each other's grief or lack of it and the conflict that arose based on those assumptions (which were all incorrect).

what the research says

It is not at all unusual for women to suffer acute feelings of sadness, anxiety, and guilt following a loss of pregnancy. Some women are at risk for full-blown depressive illnesses after a miscarriage. The symptoms extend far beyond grief and sadness to things like marked changes in eating and sleeping, loss of energy and interests, problems with concentration and memory, persistent low mood, feelings of worthlessness, and possible preoccupation with thoughts of death and suicide. Women who develop this set of symptoms have moved beyond the "Of course you feel bad, you had a miscarriage" stage into a condition that requires treatment. Fortunately, treatment for depression is extremely effective. Women are at greater risk of developing clinical depression if they have had a depressive episode in their lives. Repeatedly failed infertility treatments and recurrent miscarriage also increase risk.

Having the experience of one miscarriage doesn't make a subsequent one any easier. There is, of course, an enormous difference between having a child and not having a child, and repeated miscarriages are most stressful for childless couples. The enormous technology and sophistication in infertility treatment is often a wonder in the lives of many couples. But infertility treatments require enormous commitment: intrusive medical procedures and treatments, significant financial resources for which there is no insurance coverage, the emotional toll of investing so much and getting so little. When miscarriage results after the physically and emotionally draining infertility treatment it can be especially difficult, particularly if a couple has been through multiple procedures.

observing pregnancy loss

The lack of formal rituals that kick in automatically in many kinds of loss is a challenge to the mourning of miscarriage. It is difficult in the midst of acute pain to be organized, creative, and energetic—all the things you need when you have to provide your own structure for observing your grief. Fortunately, understanding of miscarriage has begun to move beyond its limited definition as a medical "event." There is growing recognition that it is also a spiritual event, an event that shakes couples' perceptions of the way the world works, that makes women feel betrayed by their bodies.

Observance of a miscarriage can happen in a church or a living room, surrounded by family and friends or alone. It can be structured with readings and songs or experienced in silence. It can occur immediately or a month or a year later. What matters is that it fills the need many people have to acknowledge the existence of this child, the dreams connected to it, the broken bonds, and the gift of connection. Some parents want a lasting symbol of the lost child. They plant gardens or trees. They use artwork or writing that express the experience in ways words cannot. Sometimes they preserve something they may associate with that child. For others, the comfort may come from their spirituality, from the structure provided by religion. They may use scripture verses, poetry, and songs to share their mourning with friends. My all-girl Catholic high school just dedicated a memorial garden for the lost children of the alumnae.

After several miscarriages occurred in our small church community, several women decided to organize a religious service for "lost children." I still remember the cover of the program: "Rachel weeps, for her children are no more." The diversity of the people attending was amazing. There were three couples with recent miscarriages, but then there were older couples who had lost children decades before. There was a woman mourning a recent abortion and a woman who had given up a child for adoption many years before. A couple in which the husband was Jewish told us about the ritual of placing stones on the graves of the dead. We used stones they brought in the ceremony, and placed them on the altar when we left. Several women suffering the agonies of infertility attended also. Within the loose structure, there was room for each of us who wanted to tell our stories. I cried a lot. But it was the kind of crying that recycles pain into something else. We tend to think of crying as an expression of weakness, but the tears that were wept that night also came from tremendous strength.

Other people may find help and support from the numerous informational and support groups— locally and nationally. These organizations often provide helpful information on the Internet, allow for conversation with other people going through similar losses, and often allow women or couples to meet others who have been through pregnancy loss.

For some women the greatest comfort is in the solitary. Or perhaps a friend who's "been there" can be a good sounding board. We also need to acknowledge that there is so much we don't understand about the experience of miscarriage, that we have absolutely no right to think we know what will make people feel better.

I heard from Sophia something that I expect will take a lifetime to grasp. "This is a season and all seasons pass." In the good times, I really don't want to think about it. In the good times I think, "Yeah, I know that." But in the hard times, in the mean times, I'm lucky if I can keep enough of her words in my head to find their comfort and wisdom. And in those small moments when I'm able, I come closer to understanding that we're not supposed to get over loss. We're supposed to go through it. Sometimes it helps to have company along the way. Sophia was good company.

Martha Manning, a writer and clinical psychologist, won the Stephen Logan Award in 1999 from the National Alliance for the Mentally Ill as a psychologist who made significant contributions to unraveling brain disorders. In 1996, she won the American Psychiatric Association's Presidential Award for Patient Advocacy. As a regular columnist for *Salt of the Earth* magazine, Manning received numerous awards from both the Associated Church Press and the Catholic Press Association. In 1995, *People* magazine listed her first novel, *Undercurrents*, as one of ten books that year worth note. And in 1997, USA TODAY chose *Chasing Grace* as a "Best Bet." Manning and her husband, Brian Depenbrock, live in Virginia. They have one child.